Changing Times

poems by

Adele Kearney

Finishing Line Press
Georgetown, Kentucky

Changing Times

ACKNOWLEDGMENTS

I acknowledge with thanks the publishers of three of these poems: Second
Nature, *Poetry USA;* Mr. Stevens' Dictation, *Plexus*; There, There, Oakland,
Sacramento News and Review; and my reviewers Marie and Kathleen Kearney,
Margaret Marshall, and Ellen Schwartz; and Tom Kearney and Tristan Burns for
help with the photos.

Publisher: Leah Maines

Editor: Christen Kincaid

Author Photo: Margaret Marshall

Cover Design: Elizabeth Maines McCleavy

Printed in the USA on acid-free paper.
Order online: www.finishinglinepress.com
                    also available on amazon.com

Author inquiries and mail orders:
Finishing Line Press
P. O. Box 1626
Georgetown, Kentucky 40324
U. S. A.

Contents

Hoy, Daddy!

I can't remember many words you said.
I remember you were in the Quartermaster
Corps because you knew something about horses.
Stories you told of the Great War in France
fell silent when my listening grandfather
and uncle died, and we children forgot all but two,
the one about being holed up in a wine cellar overnight,
and the one about you and another private making your
sergeant operate the handcar. Now we think that was
highly unlikely, but I guess that's why it was a story.
You always recited Ride a Cock Horse
while dandling the youngest on your good leg,
the one not hurt in the mine.
You let me sit on that good knee, too,
to hear the Sunday comics—
Blondie, Bringing Up Father,
and the Katzenjammer Kids.
You could recite what you memorized
in grade school (your only school)—
The Wreck of the Hesperus, The Village
Blacksmith, the presidents in order, the states and
capitals. And you could say hello and count to ten
in languages you learned from other men in the mines,
Italian, Polish, Magyar, or from the French in France.
Much later, when I would come home from a distance
to visit, I would be surprised again at your country speech
(Irish country, or Pennsylvania hillbilly?).
When you called to one of us, it was "Hoy!"
I can't remember that you ever spoke to me of
your love for me, but even now you're long gone
I count on its strength.
Hoy, Daddy, hoy!

Grandpap Murtha

What we three older children knew of your love:
pipe, rocking chair (horses and carriage, fast),
the ready gifts of paper and pencil stubs,
your kind blue gaze through our first years, your last.
The American Store sold us your tobacco
and gave us back a penny from your dime
you let us keep. With your retirement watch you
taught us Roman numbers, how to tell time.
Tom Mix (Jim) and his friend (Marie) rode at full tilt.
Rocker overturned, Jane's (my) fall was bad.
I don't recall your likely Irish lilt,
maybe like country tones of our own dad.
I could say I briefly, barely knew you.
but the gateway to my life was through you.

Changing Times:
Adeline Murtha Kearney

Two pictures show how times changed in your youth.
One shows you in a modest black lace dress,
with your long hair ratted, bouffant.
The next, after you asked your older brothers if you
should bob your hair, and they said okay,
shows you as a proud flapper, self-possessed.

Your dad, who worked on the coke ovens,
helped build St. Joseph's school.
You were like him, tall, like him, unlike
your petite mother, married at sixteen
to her family's boarder, ten years older.

Mary Anne raised six sons and three daughters,
sold eggs to add to their income,
was expert at all women's work, all kinds of needlework,
knitting, crochet, embroidery, and taught her daughters.
The quilting frames were always up in her house.

You never really liked the name Mary Anne found for you,
her youngest daughter. Mary Anne read it in a newspaper.
She wrote *Adaline*, rhymed it with *in*.
The rest of the world copied the song "Sweet Adeline,"
never spelled it right, rhymed it with *wine*.
You took Regina for your confirmation name.

The pastor of St. Joseph's parish said that,
if seventh graders had higher scores than eighth graders on the
same final tests, then they should graduate too.
That's how you finished high school at sixteen.

Your friends complained that you missed things.
They said you always had to go home
to help your mother with the canning.

Mary Anne said no, you couldn't accept a job
playing piano for silent films at the Grand.
Then you trimmed hats at a millinery store.
You said it was the best job you ever had.

You had six brothers, two much older sisters.
The nun, Sister Theodosia, or Nell,
got you a first-from-this-town scholarship,
to her own all-girl college, Seton Hill.
Your mother made you quit
after two years. She was afraid that
you, who so loved babies, might want to be a nun.
You became a teacher. Teachers
 needed only two years of college then.

Catholics were not allowed to teach in the town's public schools.
You got a job teaching in the township,
a consolidated school with the first three grades
and as many as seventy pupils.
It was a streetcar ride, then a long walk.

The Murthas moved. Main Street, a large brick house, with
Italian marble fireplaces, a double house shared with Uncle John.
Soon after, Mary Anne, not yet sixty, died.
Chris Kearney, or Christ (rhyming with kissed) on his
driver's license, came to the wake. His parents
knew your dad from Shercock, Ireland.
After that, Chris would pick you up from school. He asked you to
marry him and be the mother of his children. You agreed.

You honeymooned at the American Legion celebration
of the Tenth-Year Great War Anniversary
in Paris. Then London, where someone said "wrong church"
when you genuflected. Then Shercock, first from your
families to return to Ireland in your generation.

Married, you moved in with Grandpap, because Uncle Jim
said he was lonely. Your first baby, Marie, was born at the end
of June, Jim the next July, both deliveries very long and hard,
anesthetics forbidden by the doctor.
The doctor advised you not to have any more children.
You consulted the parish priest. You had five more.

You worked hard, kept house near perfection, had paid help
except during the next world war, and your girls helped.
You corrected our grammar, never showed off your Latin or German.
Grandpap's, then Dad's, garden produced, and you canned, a lot.
You trained morning glories to climb strings beside the back porch.
Once, when you thought Chris pruned the mock
orange blossom bush too close to the ground, you cried.

1929. The Depression. Our mines closed. Prohibition ended.
Chris, with his savings, bought a beer distributor license and trucks.
You did the heavy bookkeeping until you had your last child
of seven (plus three orphaned cousins, Jack Murtha, and
Ed and Bud Kearney, who sometimes lived with us).
Then Fran Ferrell from the bank came to the house weekly.
All the boys were paperboys, sorted beer bottles, and drove
delivery trucks. The girls helped out with the chores
and learned knitting and embroidery from you.
But you never asked us to help you with the canning.

Adeline the Teacher

In a strike, the mine brought
black workers up from the South.
So you had black children in your school.
You told us you always said it was
not fair the blacks were charged higher rents.

Their children had never been to school.
Israel, seventeen, couldn't read but could light your
potbellied stove. You said: "Israel, you're so good
with your hands. You should work with your hands."
Israel said: "I don't want to work with my hands,
Miss Murtha. I want to learn to read." And he did.

Waste Glass

The hollow just below the factory
was heaped with leavings of the hand-blown glass
in every shape and color.
They were our rubies and our emeralds,
our mines of Africa, pirates' treasure,
Aladdin's jeweled fruit, renewed by
magic every day. We played there,
trading riches, our pockets heavy
with imaginings.

Sister Jean Marie Makes the Rules

She was the short round one
with a dependable grin
On her red face, grated like Peggoty's,
I thought when I read David Copperfield
behind my fifth-grade arithmetic.
If she saw, she never said.
She wasn't one to fuss, had no favorites,
dealt as evenly with the
precocious youngest girl
as with slow boys older, bigger,
just waiting for school-leaving age.
It was the Depression.
Many parents, former miners,
were unemployed.
When the truck came round
with surplus food,
we all got gallon cans
of loganberries.
To get the real prizes,
in short supply, we played a game.
Guess what number Sister was thinking of.
I never won a ham, and I was slow to
understand the certain special justice
she decreed. From each as they can,
to each as they need.

Hunting Violets

H.C. Frick Coke and Coal owned the company houses
and even the underground beneath our house.
But we reclaimed the vacant lots
and fields. We had our hunting seasons
and preserves. In spring, the girls
in twos and threes invaded the old
institute to hunt for violets hiding
at the foot of trees.
We brought back big bunches, inches
across, to take to school in
mustard jars, for the May altar
in a back corner of the classroom.
If it was your turn, you wove
a tiny crown for Mary.

Second Nature

*"Women, in general, want to be loved for what they are
and men for what they accomplish. The first for their looks
and charm, the later for their action."*—Theodore Reich

Bonsai:
Late to uncage her—
quaint denatured dwarf within
limits perfected.

Espalier:
Let go the rack now?
He hugs the wall, barely holds
the overripe fruit.

Pretty Names

The miners and their sons
had plain old names,
English names of Roman saints,
John, Thomas, James,
sturdy proof of their existence
when they were away all day
at the mines,
solid, like Egyptian statuary,
to survive the cave-in.
But the women and sometimes
their towns
had pretty names,
Mary Kate, Mary Margaret, Patricia,
reminders of the home country,
the recurring blossom
before the recurring blight.
Called one Kitty, who left
no descendants.
It was sin to choose
her life or her child's.
Called her Mary Anne,
the tiny, graceful girl
who bore twelve babies,
buried three,
worked harder,
died young.
Borrowed names from France,
called her Marie, Adele.
Lived in the shadow of the slag heap
in the ugly town
called Marguerite,
to sweeten the bitter ash
where no grass grew.
Lived in what was, before our time,

nicknamed Hell Town,
officially named Mount Pleasant,
meaning, the sign said,
a pleasant hill.
Worked in the grimy town
called Donora,
where in 1948
smoke mixed with fog
to kill and borrow a new word from London,
smog, to name the bleak truth
pretty names cannot disguise.

More than Three Miles to Go

From the Three Mile Hill above our town,
at night, you could see below
nine hundred ninety-nine beehive ovens in rows,
like giant strings of glowing beads
warming the horizon of our world.
My mother's father, like my dad's,
worked there, leveling coke.
Her brothers helped with the daubing
when they were too young to work for pay.
They did all right for themselves.
One became the yard boss of that famous
one-less-than-one-thousand
while the good times lasted.
He didn't last much longer,
by turns placating and defying
the ulcerous inheritance of upward mobility
with his Luckies and his highballs and his Tums.
And, one cold New Year's Eve,
he gambled on one more good time and lost,
let it all bleed away.
Another lost a leg to an oven
but still worked round them all his life,
following the slag heaps when they moved
closer to the river for cheap freight,
and left our red brick beehives cold and dark
and cupboards not near full enough
to keep the town's sons at their father's sides.
No one consoled themselves
thinking of lives saved.
Talk about Three Mile Island
to Mrs. Burns, whose son-in-law
had to go that far, clear across the state,
to find good work, she only says:
I buried my Walter with black lung.

You can't say coal is any better.
My mother, so sure a barometer
she could reliably replace elections,
is hard put to take a stand,
still puzzled by the stunning apparition
of her sister, Sister Theodosia,
captured by a TV camera
at a demonstration against pollution.
(But, she explains, Nell had bad lungs herself.)
And she quotes an even older woman
she heard at the beauty shop.
It used to be, when the smoke blew from the west,
we knew it was the Morewood ovens.
When it came from the east,
we knew it was Carpentertown.
We didn't call it pollution then,
We called it prosperity.

The Streets of Rome

I hold dear in my heart the happy fact
that I once walked the ancient streets of Rome
my eyes sometimes surprised by small stone plaques
to Englishmen who made these streets their home.

The streets of Rome are neither long nor wide
but they are carved deep with antiquity.
Fountains, columns, statues on every side,
stained glass, flowers, mark the marble city.

Joyce walked here, as Shelley did before. Then,
near the Spanish Steps, sickly young Keats came,
faced fears, longing. But soon he died, again
in despair of love and of his own fame.

He was loved and of all men should have known
a thing of beauty is a joy forever.
And I, so lucky to know Keats and Rome,
take heed: Live this hour now; despair never.

Via Rasella

On a Sunday walk in Rome
I met a woman, Ruth, who came,
for all her foreign accent, from home,
from California.
We walked all morning and exclaimed
when some medieval lane
burst open on the fame
of a Renaissance piazza.

Her eyes skimmed shops and monuments
while her voice with its odd dissonance
went on about the incidents
of her sad scene then.
Her husband had so often lied,
never said he had a child,
a troubled girl who later tried
to come between them.

I was feeling ill at ease.
I interrupted. You have to see
this spot—Via Rasella—please.
It was March, 1944.
This is where the partisans'
hidden bomb killed marching Germans
(Tyrol draftees who spoke German),
right here, the last year of the war.

Roman soldiers could only do
what German orders told them to.
They lined up men they found at home
outside Palazzo Barberini.
Orders rose up the ranks until
the last order was Hitler's will:
Shoot ten for each German killed.
They set Via Rasella men free.

They looked but found very few
condemned in prison. They knew,
following orders, what they had to do.
No way the lives could be saved.
The army decided that they would round
up leftists in jail or out and they found
also men of Jewish background,
took them to the Ardeantine Caves.

The Jews numbered seventy-five,
their only crime: to be alive.
They took them in, in groups of five,
shot each in the back of the head.
Two hundred sixty Romans, I told her,
plus Jews, so that must mean then that there were
five extra but that would never deter
killers from shooting them all dead.

Rome put up statues at the palace gate;
at first, wreaths each year to commemorate
the Romans, near their homes, and at the caves
a service for the Romans killed.
Without a moment's pause to mention
how little I held her attention
Ruth went on with her narration,
a story with bitterness filled.

Just before her husband left her,
a week ago, she found a letter.
The daughter wrote she felt much better
now she had met her father's new girlfriend.
That same day, they called and said
they had found the daughter dead
her own bullet through her head.
Ruth was not sorry and could not pretend.

And I could only stammer pity
for everyone whose hidden grief
no city honors with a wreath.
I tried to tell her:
No history finds room to trace
the dark and complicated ways
by which we come from some home place
to Via Rasella.

Mr. Stevens' Dictation

"Is the function of the poet here mere sound,
subtler than the ornatest prophecy
to stuff the ear?"… Wallace Stevens

Every morning, he walked to work.
Maybe first he kissed the cool beauty still in bed,
the model of Liberty on the Mercury dime,
and after his unhurried breakfast,
had a kind word for the maid.
As he walked, he set in flight one of his
aerodynamic models, one of many
variations on a theme.
Their virtuoso wit still hangs in the mist.
Under the arching rainbow question,
what is real?,
his Alhambra answer shimmers:
Only I and my artifice endure.
At the office, probably he found
his private secretary ready for
the dictation of his poems.
It was a work of love.
She never minded the long
reworking of the work.
How marvelous, she might think.
This Vice President, keeping aloft
all those years, all those ethereal
products of the actuarial vault,
lighter than air.
But did he sometimes,
when his private secretary
was out sick, have to send
revisions to the steno pool?

Did some typist, not so humble
as her station,
let his writings wait for days,
while she was sneaking in
her own scribblings
of her own life,
pretty sure what was real,
and thinking more how she could change it?
A sputter in the steno pool.
A Kitty Hawk.

**Meeting Edna O'Brien
in the Sunday Magazine**

We know you would have earrings, gold, that pierce
your flesh. You wear a necklace, a remembrance
maybe, and a sign to some one reader.
Wanton, curly hair. It's red, they say,
somewhat fierce, still or again not gray.
Plucked brows, lips for once not laughing,
Cheekbones catching shadow.
No red petticoat, a light sweater set.
I imagine it gray-green like your eyes,
your wronged eyes, refusing to not look
but strained by seeing. Your fine, dainty head,
tilted with humor, question, weariness,
on your strong neck, a lot like your brother's
a little lined, a little red, unbowed.

To Patrick Kavenagh

By luck, I came upon your stilly waters—
choked with scum and bottles—no ships from Athy,
and yet—clear water shoots from under
and breaks the heavy silence of July.
A little river rat stares back at me,
paws clasped, as if to beg. I think it mocks
the poet's pose of not seeking meals or money,
only deep truth or beauty. Near your lock,
I rest and honor you, who took little note
of women's equal hunger. Still, honest, steady—
you did so much. You did not drown—or float—
or hero-like avoid each wrong-way eddy.
But you got clear—you shot the falls and broke
the choking silence of a century.

When Kay Boyle Died

On New Year's Day, in ninety-three
I walked around Lake Merritt.
I saw her in the birds there,
in their skill and grace, as if she
had won the power of flight and birdsong.
She poured out to the world her words
and still found time for action,
joining in to push the world on,
to push as hard as she could,
time for needling satire,
time for husbands and six children.
I never had noticed the feet of the birds,
how they flexed and retracted,
how they braced for landing,
searched out and curled around a branch,
the strong slim underpinnings of
the flight and song.

There, There, Oakland

That quisling
quotation,

Gertrude Stein's
stuttering stare

at her
childhood city,

is more famous
than fair.

Wryly
right,

cloudy,
not clear,

the tricky
truth translates:

her old home
wasn't here.

To old Miwok tribes
and new global blends,

Oakland is rare,
beyond compare.

Green oaks, blue skies,
tidal lake: They're all there,
there. **So there.**

Grandpap's Flowers

When in a reverie about the past
I call to mind Grandpap's plants in our yard,
I think I know them all from first to last
that stretched past grape arbor to the old barn.
From the back porch morning glories would rise
above maybe an orange petunia bed.
Looking down from the porch, on the right,
above the little hill, a rose bush, red.
A little lower, left, the mock orange
blossom, with leaves for money in our play,
below, more roses, lilies, peonies,
opposite right, French lilacs, one big bouquet.
Below it, more roses, jonquils, flag lilies,
All joined in spring by blossoms from fruit trees.

Hollyhock

Just across from Grandpap's well-tended yard
on Main Street in my family's home town
there was a lot full of rock and brick shards,
vacant because the Cooper House burned down.
We pried up lozenges of white marble
from pieces left there of the lobby floor.
We made paths through the high, dry grass jungle
where we played Tarzan or took sides for war.
Beside the ruined lobby, untended,
grew some tall pink, red, and white hollyhocks.
We learned how a yellow stamen upended
Looked like a dancer's top above her frock.
Vacant lot and Frick Park across the way
were two places we found neighbors to play.

Queen Anne's Lace

The vacant lot had still other delights
back in Mount Pleasant, our home place.
One was the sturdy green and airy white
of the wild carrot called Queen Anne's lace.
The English queen who made her impression
is the Queen Anne the war is named after
or the War of the Spanish Succession.
That Anne was King James the Second's daughter,
succeeding William and Mary. She saved
their Irish colony, with many battles—
maybe not much loved in the Irish State.
When I saw its lace in Ireland and prattled
to the Irish if we came upon it,
why did they not know what name was on it?

Huntington Library's Chinese Garden

A lake, a teahouse, and a granite bridge
adorn this garden. You will find nowhere
but in China such a garden this big.
Whole lotus and camellia plants compare
so closely to those found in their old home.
Yet the great wealth that build the library
came from the Central Pacific Railroad
through the Sierras and across the prairie
built by back-breaking work, mostly by Chinese
who could not be citizens or buy land.
Money for the teahouse, flowers, and trees
came from well-off Chinese-Americans
plus that from Huntington, from the railway,
(or from poor Chinese workers, you might say).

Hyacinths

They say hyacinths come from the eastern
Mediterranean, even Iran.
I imagine them in Iraq, Lebanon,
or the hanging gardens of Babylon.
Hyacinths symbolize resurrection,
whether from the myth that says Apollo
killed a boy and reincarnated him,
or a bulb's magic bloom from dark hollows.
My country was the source of many bombs
that rained on these lands that so lack real rain.
My wish is that all mad bombs will now stop.
War gone, may food and flowers grow again,
May hyacinths adorn our obsequies
to welcome peace and calm after tragedy.

Dave and Caitlin Together

What should we wish these two who join their hearts
and hands here? Their eyes were, it must be true,
drawn to each other from the first moment
her Irish green met his half-Irish blue.

(I think they must have felt close at first sight—
because they fit as if meant to be one,
as if far distant transAtlantic paths
join now their single voyages are done.)

He helps heal veterans; she smooths translations.
They both love books, music, and hiking the northwest.
They keep friends and family close and still find
some way to give their work the very best.

I was one of those who could never hide
my approval of their match, long before
they got engaged. I couldn't be more pleased
with this island wedding by the seashore.

So it is with much pleasure, full of hope,
I wish them long life, in their new family,
With an enduring happiness as great
as friends and family feel for them today.

Mama Boots

When I saw you slinking to my great surprise
through the slim slit of the unlocked shed door,
I glimpsed tuxedo fur, white legs, and yellow eyes.

Next day, remembering, I thought it wise
to check to see what you were headed for
when I saw you slinking to my great surprise.

In the shed, I saw more than I'd surmised:
eight blue eyes plus small white boots on the floor,
well guarded by your blazing yellow eyes.

With lots of help, I transferred all you five
to Happy Tails rescue, who kept your four,
and returned you, content, to my surprise—

A spayed, tame, happy pet cat, home at nights;
days, flirting in yard and beyond, outdoors,
with your wild mate's white boots and yellow eyes.

You got sick. Phone calls didn't get a rise
out of your vet. Thought next day, I'll try some more.
Then I saw you sink down to my great surprise,
stiff legs, and blank, your dear, once yellow eyes.

Turnabout
(To my daughter Margaret)

I held you, my baby, in my arms,
enchanted with your baby charms,
and sang along with the radio.
"Que sera, sera,
whatever will be, will be.
The future's ours mine to see,
Que sera, sera."
You were the sweetest fixture
in my life. Singing to you,
I made us both happy.
If I thought about the words,
I thought life was a mixture
of fate and chance and will.
And I think so still.
The best of life
is to be close to another.
How lucky I am that it's
turning out
turnabout
now you more often are the one
holding me.

Adele Kearney was born on April 7, 1931, in Mount Pleasant, Pennsylvania. She attended Seton Hill College in Greensburg, Pennsylvania, for two years before moving to Washington, D.C., in 1950 to work for the FBI while taking night school classes at George Washington University. She graduated in 1953 and taught third grade for a year in Rockville, Maryland, then moved to California, where she studied at Stanford University. She was a technical writer for IBM for thirty years, including a year and a half at IBM Rome. She had one daughter and was active in the civil rights movement and the California Peace and Freedom Party. She died in Sacramento on September 30, 2016, heeding to the end the advice in the last line of her poem "The Streets of Rome": "Live this hour now; despair never." *Changing Times* is her first poetry collection.